Rookie Read-About® Science

What's the Difference?
Frogs and Toads

by Lisa M. Herrington

Content Consultant
Dr. Lucy Spelman

Reading Consultant
Jeanne M. Clidas, Ph.D.
Reading Specialist

Children's Press®
An Imprint of Scholastic Inc.

Library of Congress Cataloging-in-Publication Data

Herrington, Lisa M., author.
  Frogs and toads / by Lisa M. Herrington.
     pages cm. -- (Rookie read-about science. What's the difference)
  Summary: "Introduces the reader to frogs and toads."-- Provided by publisher.
  ISBN 978-0-531-21484-8 (library binding) -- ISBN 978-0-531-21532-6 (pbk.)
1. Frogs--Juvenile literature. 2. Toads--Juvenile literature. 3. Children's questions and answers. I. Title.

  QL668.E2H4435 2016
  597.8--dc23   2015017324

Produced by Spooky Cheetah Press
Design by Keith Plechaty

Printed in China 62

1 2 3 4 5 6 7 8 9 10 R 25 24 23 22 21 20 19 18 17 16

Photographs ©: cover left: Minden Pictures/Superstock, Inc.; cover right: Fabrizio Moglia/Getty Images; 3 top left: Rolf Nussbaumer/image/imageBroker/Superstock, Inc.; 3 top right: NaturePL/Superstock, Inc.; 3 bottom: kikkerdirk/Thinkstock; 4 top: Fablok/Shutterstock, Inc.; 4 bottom: PanStock/Shutterstock, Inc.; 7 top: Fablok/Shutterstock, Inc.; 7 bottom: PanStock/Shutterstock, Inc.; 8: Cordier Sylvain/Hemis/Corbis Images; 11: Paul Reeves Photography/Shutterstock, Inc.; 12: Arvind Balaraman/Shutterstock, Inc.; 15: Luis Quinta/Nature Picture Library; 16 top: Michael Rolands/Shutterstock, Inc.; 16 bottom: Dirk Ercken/Shutterstock, Inc.; 19 top: Mark Bowler/Science Source; 19 bottom: Photo Fun/Shutterstock, Inc.; 20 top: Timescape/Dreamstime; 20 bottom: Simon Colmer/Nature Picture Library; 23 top: Animals Animals/Superstock, Inc.; 23 bottom: FLPA/Superstock, Inc.; 24 inset: Thomas Marent/Visuals Unlimited/Corbis Images; 25 top inset: Nature Picture Library/Alamy Images; 25 bottom inset: M G Therin Weise/Media Bakery; 26: Arvind Balaraman/Shutterstock, Inc.; 27: Piotr Wawrzyniuk/Shutterstock, Inc.; 28 top left: Audrey Snider-Bell/Shutterstock, Inc.; 28 top right: Cyril Papot/Shutterstock, Inc.; 28 bottom: reptiles4all/Shutterstock, Inc.; 29 top left: Aleksey Stemmer/Shutterstock, Inc.; 29 top right: Dirk Ercken/Dreamstime; 29 bottom: Fuse/Thinkstock; 30: Paul Reeves Photography/Shutterstock, Inc.; 31 top: Michael Rolands/Shutterstock, Inc.; 31 center top: Timescape/Dreamstime; 31 center bottom: Jupiterimages/Thinkstock; 31 bottom: Arvind Balaraman/Shutterstock, Inc.

Map by XNR Productions, Inc.

Table of Contents

4

Which Is Which?

They both have long, sticky tongues to catch bugs. They are amphibians (am-FIB-ee-uhns). That means they live in water and on land. But which is the frog and which is the toad?

Did you guess right? Frogs and toads are a lot alike. But they are not exactly the same. There are ways to tell them apart.

frog

feet

skin
type

length
of legs

toad

7

Slimy Skin, Dry Skin

What is one way to tell a frog from a toad? You would have to touch them to feel the difference!

Frogs have slimy, moist skin. It can dry out quickly. They spend a lot of time in the water to keep their skin wet.

Toads have dry, rough skin. It is covered with bumps that look like warts. A toad's skin does not dry out as quickly as a frog's skin does. Toads spend more time on land than in water.

webbed feet

Different Bodies

Most frogs have a long, thin body. They also have long back legs. A frog's thin body and long legs are great for leaping and swimming. Many frogs have **webbed** feet to help them swim.

FUN FACT!

Some frogs can jump 20 times their body length. That is like you being able to jump the length of two school buses!

Most toads have round bodies and short back legs. A toad cannot jump far. It walks and hops. Most toads do not have webbed feet. They usually do not swim.

A European toad walks through the forest.

This frog uses camouflage to hide among plants in a pond.

The bright color of this strawberry poison arrow frog tells enemies to stay away!

Staying Safe

Predators, such as snakes, birds, and raccoons, like to eat frogs and toads. But both animals know how to stay safe.

Many frogs blend in with their surroundings. This **camouflage** makes it hard for enemies to see them.

Some frogs have poison in their skin. Their skin may be bright red, yellow, or blue. The bright colors warn predators to stay away!

Many toads also use camouflage to stay safe from enemies. They may blend in with leaves on the forest floor.

Toads have a lump behind each eye. The lumps contain poisonous glands. Predators know the poison will make them sick.

FUN FACT!

Some toads and frogs can puff up so they look too big to swallow. This scares away snakes and other animals.

Cane toads have very large poisonous glands.

Can you find the toad hidden in the leaves?

19

frog eggs

toad eggs

Growing Up

Most frogs and toads start their lives as eggs. The eggs are laid in water or moist areas.

Frogs lay their eggs in big **masses**.

Most toads lay their eggs in long chains.

Tadpoles hatch from both frog and toad eggs. The tadpoles look like fish. They have tails and no legs. Tadpoles use their gills to breathe underwater. Later, lungs replace the gills so they can breathe air on land. Their tails shrink away. They grow four legs. They become adult frogs and toads.

Now you know the difference between these animal look-alikes!

frog tadpoles

toad tadpoles

23

Frogs and toads live everywhere in the world except Antarctica. They even make their homes in cold places and deserts.

North America

The **glass frog** is named for its see-through belly. It lives in Central and South America.

South America

MAP KEY

Range of frogs and toads

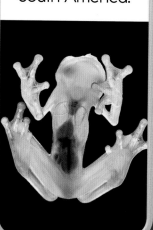

Around the World

A **European toad** uses its tongue to catch small prey. It grabs larger animals in its jaws.

Europe

Asia

Africa

Australia

The **tomato frog** is found only in Madagascar. It puffs itself up to keep predators away.

Antarctica

webbed feet

long back legs
for jumping
and swimming

slimy, wet skin

long, thin body

lays eggs
in groups

frog

Difference?

dry, rough, bumpy skin

round body

short back legs for walking and hopping

usually does not have webbed feet

lays eggs in long chains

toad

Frogs come in a rainbow of colors!

tomato frog

blue poison arrow frog

golden dart frog

Amazing!

red-eyed
tree frog

red-striped
poison dart frog

orange mantella frog

Guess Who?

- ✓ My skin is rough and bumpy.
- ✓ Short legs let me walk and hop.
- ✓ I lay my eggs in long chains.

Am I a frog or a toad?

Answer: toad

Glossary

camouflage (KAM-uh-flahzh): coloring or covering that makes animals look like their surroundings

masses (MASSES): large number of things piled together

predators (PRED-uh-turs): animals that eat other animals

webbed (WEBBED): having skin connecting the toes of an animal

Index

Facts for Now

Visit this Scholastic Web site for more information
on frogs and toads:
www.factsfornow.scholastic.com
Enter the keywords **Frogs and Toads**

About the Author

Lisa M. Herrington has written many books and articles about
animals for kids. She lives in Trumbull, Connecticut, with her husband,
Ryan, and daughter, Caroline.

32